Draw Near with Faith

A Confirmation Prayer Book

compiled by

GEOFFREY SHILVOCK

Priest-in-charge of Christ Church, Malvern

MOWBRAY
LONDON & OXFORD

ISBN 0 264 67001 9

First published 1984
by A.R. Mowbray & Co. Ltd,
Saint Thomas House, Becket Street,
Oxford, OX1 1SJ

Typeset by Fourjay Typesetters, Oxford
Printed in Great Britain by The Eastern Press Limited

Contents

Acknowledgements

Extracts from the Book of Common Prayer of 1662, which is Crown Copyright, are reproduced by permission of Eyre & Spottiswoode, Her Majesty's Printers, London.

The Collects from Morning and Evening Prayer, together with other prayers from The Alternative Service Book 1980, are © the Central Board of Finance of the Church of England and are reproduced with permission.

The Apostles' Creed and the Lord's Prayer, in its modern form, are © International Consultation on English Texts.

Two extracts from *New Every Morning* (1974) are used by permission of BBC Publications.

Thirteen Psalms (or part thereof) from *The Psalms: a new translation for worship* © English text 1976, 1977 David L. Frost, John A. Emerton, Andrew A. Macintosh are used by permission of Wm Collins Sons & Co. Ltd.

Foreword

by the Rt Revd Philip Goodrich, Bishop of Worcester

It is generally recognized that the care and instruction of Confirmation candidates after their Confirmation is every bit as important as their preparation beforehand. This book of prayers will be of great help to communicants, young and old, precisely because it is practical and down-to-earth.

I think we have left new communicants to their own devices too much, hoping that they will prepare for Communion by some instinct which they may not have. We trust too blandly that they will fill out their devotions at the Parish Communion, when in fact they and their fellow-worshippers are merely giving way to distraction and irreverent inattention.

So here is a book to reverse the trend of thoughtless worship and to help people in the first steps of learning to pray. I commend it warmly.

+ Philip Worcester

The Habit of Prayer

It is important for Christians to develop regular habits of prayer, and this little book has been devised to help Confirmation candidates and others do just that. It aims to provide a simple scheme of daily prayer as well as being a short anthology of famous and new prayers. Prayer is often best if we use our own words, however inadequate they may be, to express our own deepest concerns. However, set prayers do have a place. They can be used to start us thinking and they can often help when we cannot easily put our thoughts into words ourselves.

What is prayer?

Prayer is asking. It is realizing our dependence on God and acknowledging that all our needs can be met by him. But it is more than that. A good way of summarizing prayer is to think of the word ACTS.

Prayer is
      Adoration — showing God our love
      Confession — telling God we are sorry
    Thanksgiving — showing God our gratitude
    Supplication — asking God's help for others as well
                      as for ourselves.

This summary also reminds us that prayer should lead us

to ACT; it should change us so that we actually become an instrument of God's love in the world.

Why pray?

We only get to know people by spending time in their company, by talking to them and by listening to them. The same is true of our relationship to God. We can learn about God and what he has done in the world by reading the Bible and other books. We can only *know* God personally if we spend time with him regularly, speak with him, and listen to him. Listening is perhaps the most important. Prayer does not always need words. Sometimes we need to sit or kneel quietly thinking about a verse from the Bible or just being aware that God is with us.

Some suggestions

Find a place which is quiet, indoors or out, and where you will not be disturbed. Always be comfortable. Traditionally we kneel to pray, but you can also sit or stand. Spend a few moments quietly thinking about God and getting into a prayerful mood. Use one of the forms of prayer from the book and take your time. If you sometimes do not feel like praying, still persevere. The way we feel is not the most important. Although prayer is often a great pleasure it *is* also a duty to God and we must not overlook that.

Try different kinds of prayer like the simple 'Jesus Prayer' of the Orthodox Church. In its most common form it runs, 'Jesus, Son of God, have mercy on me a sinner'. The prayer should be repeated quietly as you breathe in and out and concentrate on God. This kind of prayer is not praying *about* anything; it is simply being in God's presence.

Experiment sometimes. Use suitable music as a background or focus your attention with a lighted candle, a cross or a picture. Use pictures of starving and destitute people taken from newspapers or magazines as you pray for those in need. Newspapers and TV should provide many of the subjects of your prayers. God is concerned about the whole world. You should be too.

Prayer is a great adventure. It will change you. Hopefully it will widen your concern for others, and it will deepen your appreciation and love of God. Once you have started to pray don't turn back, but persevere. It has many rewards for the true seeker.

Some Prayers to Learn

The Invocation

In the Name of the Father and of the Son and of the Holy Spirit. Amen

The Lord's Prayer (traditional form)

Our Father, who art in heaven,
hallowed be thy name;
thy kingdom come;
thy will be done;
on earth as it is in heaven.
Give us this day our daily bread.
And forgive us our trespasses,
as we forgive those who trespass against us.
And lead us not into temptation;
but deliver us from evil.
For thine is the kingdom, the power and the glory,
for ever and ever. Amen.

The Lord's Prayer (modern form)

Our Father in heaven,
hallowed be your name,
your kingdom come,
your will be done,
on earth as in heaven.
Give us today our daily bread.
Forgive us our sins
as we forgive those who sin against us.
Lead us not into temptation
but deliver us from evil.
For the kingdom, the power, and the glory
    are yours,
now and for ever. Amen.

The Doxology

Glory to the Father and to the Son:
    and to the Holy Spirit;
as it was in the beginning, is now
    and shall be for ever. Amen.

A Confession

I confess to God Almighty, the Father, the Son and the
Holy Spirit, that I have sinned in thought, word and
deed through my own fault. I pray God to have mercy
upon me and to forgive all my sins.

The Apostles' Creed

I believe in God, the Father almighty,
creator of heaven and earth.
I believe in Jesus Christ, his only Son,
    our Lord.
He was conceived by the power of the
    Holy Spirit
and born of the Virgin Mary.
He suffered under Pontius Pilate,
was crucified, died, and was buried.
He descended to the dead.
On the third day he rose again.
He ascended into heaven,
and is seated at the right hand
    of the Father.
He will come again to judge the living
    and the dead.
I believe in the Holy Spirit,
the holy catholic Church,
the communion of saints,
the forgiveness of sins,
the resurrection of the body,
and the life everlasting. Amen.

A General Thanksgiving

Almighty God, Father of all mercies,
we your unworthy servants give you most
    humble and hearty thanks
for all your goodness and loving kindness
to us and to all men.
We bless you for our creation, preservation,
    and all the blessings of this life;
but above all for your immeasurable love
in the redemption of the world by our
    Lord Jesus Christ,
for the means of grace, and for the hope of glory.
And give us, we pray, such a sense of all
    your mercies
that our hearts may be unfeignedly thankful,
and that we show forth your praise,
not only with our lips but in our lives,
by giving up ourselves to your service,
and by walking before you in holiness
    and righteousness all our days;
through Jesus Christ our Lord,
to whom, with you and the Holy Spirit,
    be all honour and glory,
for ever and ever. Amen.

A General Intercession

O God, the creator and preserver of all
mankind, we pray for men of every race, and in
every kind of need: make your ways known on
earth, your saving power among all nations.
(especially we pray for . . .)
Lord in your mercy
hear our prayer.

We pray for your Church throughout the world:
guide and govern us by your Holy Spirit, that
all who profess and call themselves Christians
may be led into the way of truth, and hold the
faith in unity of spirit, in the bond of peace, and
in righteousness of life. (Especially we pray for . . .)
Lord, in your mercy
hear our prayer.

We commend to your fatherly goodness all who
are anxious or distressed in mind or body;
comfort and relieve them in their need, give them
patience in their sufferings, and bring good
out of their troubles. (Especially we pray for . . .)
Merciful Father,
accept these prayers
for the sake of your Son,
our Saviour Jesus Christ. Amen.

A grace at mealtimes

Blessed are you, Lord God of all creation.
Through your goodness we receive our daily bread
which earth has given and human hands have made.
We bless you and praise you for ever. Amen.

Anima Christi (Soul of Christ)

Soul of Christ, sanctify me.
Body of Christ, save me.
Blood of Christ, fill me.
Water from the side of Christ, wash me.
Passion of Christ, strengthen me.
Good Jesus, hear me.
Do not let me be separated from you.
From the enemy defend me.
At the hour of my death call me,
That with your saints I may praise you
for ever and ever. Amen.

The Grace

The grace of our Lord Jesus Christ,
the love of God,
and the fellowship of the Holy Spirit,
be with us all, evermore. Amen.

Psalms for Daily Use

The Psalms are the hymns and prayers which Jesus used, and they have always been used widely in Christian worship. They express many human emotions such as fear, anger, love, disillusionment and hope. As we say the psalms we can bring before God all that we are and everything that we feel.

Here are two psalms for each day of the week. You could use one in the morning and one at evening. Try using other psalms when you have become familiar with these.

It is traditional to say the Doxology after each psalm.

Sunday

PSALM 121

1 I lift up my eyes to the hills:
    but where shall I find help?
2 My help comes from the Lord:
    who has made heaven and earth.
3 He will not suffer your foot to stumble:
    and he who watches over you will not sleep.
4 Be sure he who has charge of Israel:
    will neither slumber nor sleep.
5 The Lord himself is your keeper:
    the Lord is your defence upon your right hand;

6 the sun shall not strike you by day:
   nor shall the moon by night.
7 The Lord will defend you from all evil:
   it is he who will guard your life.
8 The Lord will defend your going out and your coming in
   from this time forward for evermore.

PSALM 122

1 I was glad when they said to me:
   'Let us go to the house of the Lord.'
2 And now our feet are standing:
   within your gates O Jerusalem;
3 Jerusalem which is built as a city:
   where the pilgrims gather in unity.
4 There the tribes go up, the tribes of the Lord:
   as he commanded Israel
   to give thanks to the name of the Lord.
5 There are set thrones of judgement:
   the thrones of the house of David.
6 O pray for the peace of Jerusalem:
   may those who love you prosper.
7 Peace be within your walls:
   and prosperity in your palaces.
8 For the sake of my brothers and companions:
   I will pray that peace be with you.
9 For the sake of the house of the Lord our God:
   I will seek for your good.

Monday

1 Blessed is the man who has not walked in the
      counsel of the ungodly:
  nor followed the way of sinners
  nor taken his seat amongst the scornful.
2 But his delight is in the law of the Lord:
  and on that law will he ponder day and night.
3 He is like a tree planted beside streams of water:
  that yields its fruit in due season.
4 Its leaves also shall not wither:
  and look whatever he does it shall prosper.
5 As for the ungodly it is not so with them:
  they are like the chaff which the wind scatters.
6 Therefore the ungodly shall not stand up at the
  judgement:
  nor sinners in the congregation of the righteous.
7 For the Lord cares for the way of the righteous:
  but the way of the ungodly shall perish.

1 Lord who may abide in your tabernacle:
  or who may dwell upon your holy hill?
2 He that leads an uncorrupt life
  and does the thing which is right:
  who speaks the truth from his heart
  and has not slandered with his tongue;

3 he that has done no evil to his fellow:
    nor vented abuse against his neighbour;
4 in whose eyes the worthless have no honour:
    but he makes much of those that fear the Lord;
5 he that has sworn to his neighbour:
    and will not go back on his oath;
6 he that has not put his money to usury:
    nor taken a bribe against the innocent.
7 He that does these things:
    shall never be overthrown.

Tuesday

PSALM 47

1 O clap your hands all you peoples:
    and cry aloud to God with shouts of joy.
2 For the Lord Most High is to be feared:
    he is a great King over all the earth.
3 He cast down peoples under us:
    and the nations beneath our feet.
4 He chose us a land for our possession:
    that was the pride of Jacob whom he loved.
5 God has gone up with the sound of rejoicing:
    and the Lord to the blast of the horn.
6 O sing praises sing praises to God:
    O sing praises sing praises to our King.
7 For God is the King of all the earth:
    O praise him in a well-wrought psalm.
8 God has become the King of the nations:

he has taken his seat upon his holy throne.
9 The princes of the peoples are gathered together:
    with the people of the God of Abraham.
10 For the mighty ones of the earth are become the
    servants of God:
    and he is greatly exalted.

PSALM 84

1 How lovely is your dwelling-place:
    O Lord God of hosts!
2 My soul has a desire and longing to enter the courts
    of the Lord:
    my heart and my flesh rejoice in the living God.
3 The sparrow has found her a home
  and the swallow a nest where she may lay her young:
    even your altar O Lord of hosts my King and my
    God.
4 Blessed are those who dwell in your house:
    they will always be praising you.
5 Blessed is the man whose strength is in you:
    in whose heart are the highways to Zion;
6 who going through the valley of dryness
  finds there a spring from which to drink:
    till the autumn rain shall clothe it with blessings.
7 They go from strength to strength:
    they appear every one of them before the God of
    gods in Zion.

8 O Lord God of hosts hear my prayer:
   give ear O God of Jacob.
9 Behold O God him who reigns over us:
    and look upon the face of your anointed.
10 One day in our courts is better than a thousand:
    I would rather stand at the threshold of the
      house of my God
    than dwell in the tents of ungodliness.
11 For the Lord God is a rampart and a shield
   the Lord gives favour and honour:
    and no good thing will he withhold from those
      who walk in innocence.
12 O Lord God of hosts:
    blessed is the man who puts his trust in you.

Wednesday

PSALM 6

1 O Lord rebuke me not in your indignation:
    nor chasten me in your fierce displeasure.
2 Have mercy upon me O Lord for I am weak:
    O Lord heal me for my very bones are afraid.
3 My soul also is greatly troubled:
    and you Lord how long will you delay?
4 Turn again O Lord and deliver my soul:
    O save me for your mercy's sake.
5 For in death no man remembers you:
    and who can give you thanks from the grave?

6 I am wearied with my groaning:
  every night I drown my bed with weeping
  and water my couch with my tears.
7 My eyes waste away for sorrow:
  they grow dim because of all my enemies.
8 Away from me all you that do evil:
  for the Lord has heard the voice of my weeping.
9 The Lord has heard my supplication:
  the Lord will receive my prayer.
10 All my enemies shall be put to shame and greatly
      dismayed:
  they shall turn back and be confounded
 in a moment.

PSALM 130

1 Out of the depths have I called to you O Lord:
  Lord hear my voice;
2 O let your ears consider well:
  the voice of my supplication.
3 If you Lord should note what we do wrong:
  who then O Lord could stand?
4 But there is forgiveness with you:
  so that you shall be feared.
5 I wait for the Lord my soul waits for him:
  and in his word is my hope.
6 My soul looks for the Lord:
  more than watchmen for the morning
  more I say than watchmen for the morning.

7 O Israel trust in the Lord for with the Lord
    there is mercy:
  and with him is ample redemption.
8 He will redeem Israel:
  from the multitude of his sins.

Thursday

  PSALM 23

1 The Lord is my shepherd:
  therefore can I lack nothing.
2 He will make me lie down in green pastures:
  and lead me beside still waters.
3 He will refresh my soul:
  and guide me in right pathways for his
  name's sake.
4 Though I walk through the valley of the
shadow of death I will fear no evil:
  for you are with me
  your rod and your staff comfort me.
5 You spread a table before me
in the face of those who trouble me:
  you have anointed my head with oil and my cup
  will be full.
6 Surely your goodness and loving-kindness will
  follow me all the days of my life:
  and I shall dwell in the house of the Lord
  for ever.

1 The earth is the Lord's and all that is in it:
    the compass of the world and those who
    dwell therein.
2 For he has founded it upon the seas:
    and established it upon the waters.
3 Who shall ascend the hill of the Lord:
    or who shall stand in his holy place?
4 He that has clean hands and a pure heart:
    who has not set his soul upon idols
    nor sworn his oath to a lie.
5 He shall receive blessing from the Lord:
    and recompense from the God of his salvation.
6 Of such a kind as this are those who seek him:
    those who seek your face O God of Jacob.
7 Lift up your heads O you gates
  and be lifted up you everlasting doors:
    and the King of glory shall come in.
8 Who is the King of glory?
    the Lord strong and mighty the Lord
    mighty in battle.
9 Lift up your heads O you gates
  and be lifted up you everlasting doors:
    and the King of glory shall come in.
10 Who is the King of glory?
    the Lord of hosts he is the King of glory.

Friday

1 How long O Lord will you so utterly forget me:
   how long will you hide your face from me?
2 How long must I suffer anguish in my soul
   and be so grieved in my heart day and night:
      how long shall my enemy triumph over me?
3 Look upon me O Lord my God and answer me:
   lighten my eyes lest I sleep in death;
4 Lest my enemy say 'I have prevailed against him':
   lest my foes exult at my overthrow.
5 Yet I put my trust in your unfailing love:
   O let my heart rejoice in your salvation.
6 And I will make my song to the Lord:
   because he deals so bountifully with me.

1 Have mercy on me O God in your enduring
      goodness:
      according to the fulness of your compassion blot
         out my offences.
2 Wash me thoroughly from my wickedness:
   and cleanse me from my sin.
3 For I acknowledge my rebellion:
   and my sin is ever before me.
4 Against you only have I sinned
   and done what is evil in your eyes:

so you will be just in your sentence
and blameless in your judging.

5 Surely in wickedness I was brought to birth:
    and in sin my mother conceived me.

6 You that desire truth in the inward parts:
    O teach me wisdom in the secret places
    of the heart.

7 Purge me with hyssop and I shall be clean:
    wash me and I shall be whiter than snow.

8 Make me hear of joy and gladness:
    let the bones which you have broken rejoice.

9 Hide your face from my sins:
    and blot out all my iniquities.

10 Create in me a clean heart O God:
    and renew a right spirit within me.

11 Do not cast me out from your presence:
    do not take your holy spirit from me.

12 O give me the gladness of your help again:
    and support me with a willing spirit.

13 Then will I teach transgressors your ways:
    and sinners shall turn to you again.

14 O Lord God of my salvation deliver me
    from bloodshed:
    and my tongue shall sing of your righteousness.

15 O Lord open my lips:
    and my mouth shall proclaim your praise.

16 You take no pleasure in sacrifice or I would
    give it:
    burnt offerings you do not want.

17 The sacrifice of God is a broken spirit:
      a broken and contrite heart O God you will
         not despise.
18 In your graciousness do good to Zion:
      rebuild thc walls of Jerusalem.
19 Then will you delight in right sacrifices
  in burnt-offerings and oblations:
      then will they offer young bulls up on your altar.

Saturday

PSALM 119(1)

1 Blessed are those whose way is blameless:
      who walk in the law of the Lord.
2 Blessed are those who keep his commands:
      and seek him with their whole heart;
3 those who do no wrong:
      but walk in the ways of our God.
4 For you Lord have commanded us:
      to persevere in all your precepts.
5 If only my ways were unerring:
  towards the keeping of your statutes!
6 Then I should not be ashamed:
      when I looked on all your commandments.
7 I will praise you with sincerity of heart:
      as I learn your righteous judgements.
8 I will keep your statutes:
      O forsake me not utterly.

105 Your word is a lantern to my feet:
    and a light to my path.
106 I have vowed and sworn an oath:
    to keep your righteous judgements.
107 I have been afflicted beyond measure:
    Lord give me life according to your word.
108 Accept O Lord the freewill offerings of my
       mouth:
    and teach me your judgements.
109 I take my life in my hands continually:
    yet I do not forget your law.
110 The wicked have laid a snare for me:
    but I have not strayed from your precepts.
111 Your commands are my inheritance forever:
    they are the joy of my heart.
112 I have set my heart to fulfil your statutes:
    always even to the end.

A note on Morning and Evening Prayers

These are simple outlines which can be filled in using material from other parts of the book or by using words of your own.

It is suggested that you try to do some Bible reading either in the morning or evening, or both if you have time. Rather than reading from the Bible at random, choose some of the shorter books first and read them through taking a section at a time. You may find one of the modern translations such as the Revised Standard Version, the New English Bible or the Good News Bible best, at least to start with.

Alternatively you can use one of the various schemes of Bible reading which are published. Some like those from the Bible Reading Fellowship have helpful notes.

Write to The Bible Reading Fellowship, St Michael's House, 2, Elizabeth Street, London SW1W 9RQ.

Morning Prayers

In the Name of the Father and of the Son and of the Holy Spirit. Amen

Open our eyes, O God, to your glory, that we may worship in spirit and truth, and offer you the praise of glad and thankful hearts.

(Use one of the daily Psalms and/or read a short passage from part of the Bible)

Lord have mercy upon us.
Christ have mercy upon us.
Lord have mercy upon us.

Our Father . . .

A Morning Prayer

Eternal God and Father,
you create us by your power
and redeem us by your love:
guide and strengthen us by your spirit,
that we may give ourselves in love and
service to one another and to you;
through Jesus Christ our Lord. Amen.

(This may be followed by other prayers and a meditation if there is time)

The Grace of our Lord Jesus Christ, and the Love of God, and the fellowship of the Holy Spirit be with us all evermore. Amen.

Evening Prayers

In the Name of the Father and of the Son and of the Holy Spirit. Amen

Look graciously upon us Holy Spirit, and give us for our hallowing, thoughts which pass into prayer, prayers which pass into love, and love which passes into life with Christ for ever.

(Take time to think over the past day and bring before God anything which you have said, thought or done for which you are now ashamed. Are there also things which you have omitted to do?)

I confess to God almighty, the Father, the Son and the Holy Spirit, that I have sinned in thought, word and deed through my own fault. I pray God to have mercy upon me and to forgive all my sins.

May almighty God have mercy upon me, forgive my sins and keep me in eternal life, through Jesus Christ our Lord. Amen.

(Use one of the daily Psalms and/or a short passage from the Bible.)

The Apostles' Creed

The Lord's Prayer

An Evening Prayer

Lighten our darkness,
Lord, we pray;
and in your mercy defend us
from all perils and dangers of this night;
for the love of your Son,
our Saviour Jesus Christ. Amen.

(Other prayers and a meditation may follow)

The Grace of our Lord Jesus Christ, and the Love of God, and the fellowship of the Holy Spirit be with us all evermore. Amen.

Topics for Daily Prayers

These may be used at either morning or evening prayers as a guide to your own intercessions and thanksgiving.

Sunday

Pray for:

> The mission of the Church
> Clergy, pastors, and missionaries
> The unity of the Church
> Translators and scholars of the Bible

Give thanks for:

> The work and ministry of Jesus
> His death and resurrection
> The gift of the Holy Spirit
> Christian fellowship

Monday

Pray for:

> The peace of the world
> Those in authority
> The right use of nature's resources
> Those who influence public opinion in the media

Give thanks for:

The beauty of the world
Our food and shelter
Man's ability to create and invent
Scientific and technological progress

Tuesday

Pray for:

Industry and commerce, and farming
The forces of law and order
Social services
Hospitals and schools

Give thanks for:

The opportunities of work and leisure
Voluntary services
All who maintain the order of society
The various means of communication

Wednesday

Pray for:

Family and friends
Broken marriages and homes
Local government
The local community

Give thanks for:

Our homes
The opportunities of service and friendship
The joys of human relationships
The pleasures of life

Thursday

Pray for:

The suffering
Refugees and the homeless
The hungry
Those in prison

Give thanks for:

Oxfam, Christian Aid
The Red Cross, Amnesty International
Welfare Workers
Medical missionaries

Friday

Pray for:

The sick and dying
The lonely and the anxious
The disabled
The elderly and housebound

Give thanks for:

- Hospices for the dying
- The caring professions (doctors, nurses, social workers, clergy)
- Relief organizations in the community
- Counselling services

Saturday

Pray for:

- Growth in faith and commitment
- Increased awareness of others
- A mind open to new truths
- A deeper understanding of God

Give thanks for:

- The Christian faith
- Opportunities of putting that faith into action
- My gifts and talents
- God's love of me

Preparation for Holy Communion

Sometime before going to a communion service, perhaps during the day before, it is good to prepare yourself mentally and spiritually, so that you do not receive the sacrament lightly. You will also find that by doing this you will get more from the service and appreciate it more. Here are some suggestions for you to follow.

In the name of the Father who made me,
and of the Son who died on the cross that I may
   have life,
and of the Holy Spirit who draws me to that life.
Amen.

Father, by the light of your Spirit
shine into the deepest places of my life
and help me to see where I have fallen short,
and where I have failed you.
Help me to be truly sorry,
to turn away from the darkness,
and to walk once more in the light of Christ. Amen.

5. Honour your father and mother

Respect your parents and any who have proper authority over you. Try and see the best in people and not the worst. It is best always to err on the side of charity in your estimate of others. Sometimes you will have to make the first move to end a quarrel. Love alone conquers evil and heals broken relationships. Always uphold the law.

6. You shall not kill

Respect all life, because it is God's creation. Never cause pain or suffering unnecessarily. Killing usually has its roots in hatred, bad temper, greed or jealousy. Examine these emotions in your own life. Always try to love others, even those who seem to be unlovable.

7. Do not commit adultery

We should not be afraid of our feelings and emotions, but we must not be ruled by them, especially when that leads us to 'use' other people or makes us betray those who love us. Always uphold Christian marriage. Sex is God-given, and it is a great privilege to be able to share in his work of creation, and also to demonstrate our love for another person, but if it is used merely for self-gratification it becomes hollow and emptied of its meaning. Do you always respect others as persons?

8. Do not steal

Stealing can take many forms from blatantly taking something which does not belong to you to failing to give generously to those in need. Our work is an area which needs careful examination. Do we work honestly and *earn* the wages we receive? Do we borrow without returning? Do we fill in forms (especially tax returns) honestly? Do we regard all our possessions as gifts of God? We cannot enjoy more than we need while our brother or sister is in want.

9. You shall not be a false witness

You must always try and speak truthfully. To be dishonest is to cheat yourself. Do not willingly damage another person's reputation by what you say. Be as fair as you can when speaking of others.

10. You shall not covet anything which belongs to your neighbour

Envy and covetousness lead to discontentment and greed. There is nothing wrong with ambition in itself or with a desire to improve your lot, but it is wrong when you try to reach your goal at the expense of others. Do you find pleasure and happiness in the simple pleasures of life and are you content?

Remember the prayer of Reinhold Niebuhr

God grant me the courage to change those things I can change; the serenity to accept those I cannot change; and the wisdom to know the difference.

Almighty Father, I confess that I have sinned in thought, word, and deed against you and my neighbour. I am truly sorry, pray for your forgiveness and ask for the help of your Holy Spirit in turning away from evil and taking hold once more of that new life won for me by Jesus Christ, our Lord. Amen.

It is sometimes a good idea to talk about some of the issues raised by this self examination either with a clergyman or someone else you can trust and with whom you feel confident. The Christian life is often called 'The Way', because it is like a pilgrimage. At times we need the advice and companionship of our fellow travellers.

Some prayers at Communion

(Before Communion)

Lord, I come to you,
not because I am worthy,
but because you have invited me.

You accept me as I am
with all my faults and inadequacies
so that I may be transformed by your love.

I do not come alone,
but as a member of the Christian family,
to join in this great celebration
of faith and hope.

As I receive the bread and wine,
so may I receive the strength and power
of the Holy Spirit
set free by Jesus
dying on the cross
and rising to new life.

This bread I give to you,
that you may bless it
and consecrate it as your body.
So bless the labours of our hands
which have produced it.
Accept it though it bear the smudge
of human greed and exploitation,
and eaten at the expense of others.
It is all we have to offer,
but in your hands
it can become the bread of life
nourishing our spirits.

Take this wine,
and with it our fun and laughter;
but also the excesses
which deny our humanity,
imprison and deprave us.
Consecrate our leisure,
re-create us and refresh us
with the life-blood of Christ
flowing into our lives.

(As you kneel at the altar rail)

Lord, I am not worthy that you should come under my roof;
only say the word, and I shall be made whole.

(After receiving)

I rise from this table with a thankful heart;
for sins forgiven;
for life and hope restored;
for the remembrance of Jesus' death,
and the celebration of his resurrection;
for the promise of his presence with me now and always;
and for joy in believing.

Father, take the life which I offer,
and use it in your service
in gratitude for your love of me. Amen.

(The Anima Christi *on page 15 is also suitable)*

May these hands Lord, which have received the
   sacrament
of your Body and Blood,
always be active in your service.
May these ears which have heard the words of life,
listen only to what is good.
May these eyes which have beheld your love,
look with compassion on the needs of others.
May these lips which have sung your praise,
speak words of comfort, encouragement and hope.
And may all we who have tasted this holy food,
be drawn together in the fellowship
of the Body of Christ. Amen.

(Based on the Malabar Liturgy)

Almighty God, may the words which we have heard this
day, take root in our hearts so that they may produce
within us the fruit of good living, through Jesus Christ
our Lord. Amen.

(Based on a prayer from the Book of Common Prayer*)*

The Way of the Cross

The Via Dolorosa, or Way of Sorrows, in Jerusalem, follows the path Jesus is believed to have taken to his crucifixion. For centuries Christians have traced this last journey, stopping at various points or 'stations' to meditate on the incidents surrounding our Lord's death and resurrection.

The practice developed of marking these 'stations' around the walls of churches, and it soon became a popular form of meditation and devotion. Traditionally there are fourteen or fifteen such stations, but in this simplified version there are just seven.

Take each station in turn. Try and picture the scene and imagine what it would have been like, and remember what Jesus has done for us. Use the prayers which are printed, or else use words which come to you naturally. Alternatively you can just sit or kneel in silence.

You will need a Bible for the references.

1. Jesus is condemned to death

O Saviour of the world, who by your cross and
    suffering,
redeemed the world, save us and help us.

Read carefully St Mark chapter 15 verses 6 to 15

(Pause to think about the reading)

> Lord, you were condemned to death for no crime,
> but only because people could not stand so much
>   goodness.
> They could not bear the brilliance of the light which
> you brought into the world.
>
> Strengthen all prisoners of conscience, all who are
> being tortured and imprisoned for no crime and
> without a fair trial.
>
> And help me Lord, to have courage to do and say
>   what is right,
> whatever the consequences.

2. The cross is laid on Jesus

> O Saviour of the world . . .

Read carefully St Matthew chapter 11 verses 29 to 30

(Pause to think about the reading)

> Lord, you did not shrink from the cross, but bore it
>   bravely,
> even though you did not deserve it.
> We too have our crosses to bear. Help us to accept
>   them

bravely and cheerfully in the knowledge that all suffering and pain can be transformed by love.

Be near those whose suffering brings only bitterness and resentment.

3. Jesus falls under the weight of the cross

O Saviour of the world . . .

Read carefully Romans chapter 7 verses 18 to 24

(Pause to think about the reading)

> Sometimes the cross seems too heavy for me to bear.
> The way is hard and I stumble and fall.
> I want to go on. I want to follow in your footsteps,
> but I give up the struggle.
> In your love I find forgiveness.
> In your acceptance I find renewed strength to go on.

4. Simon of Cyrene takes the cross

O Saviour of the world . . .

Read carefully St Mark 15 verse 21

(Pause to think about the reading)

> Lord, even you needed the help of a stranger
> and you accepted it willingly.

Help us to share each other's burdens and
lighten eath other's load.

So many people are weighed down under pressures;
the unemployed, the sick, the poor,
those who live in poor housing,
and those whose relationships are unhappy.
Help me like Simon, to ease their burden and support
   them
whenever I can.

5. Jesus is crucified

O Saviour of the world . . .

Read carefully St Mark chapter 15 verses 22 to 32

(Pause to think about the reading)

Lord, Man is such a violent creature sometimes.
We mar your image in us by our inhumanity to each
   other.
We hurt one another, and commit atrocities.
We fight and make war.
We threaten and exploit.

And yet in the mystery of your crucifixion;
in your forgiveness for those who killed you,
and in your promise to the thief,
you show that evil does not have the last word;
that goodness and love are stronger and can overcome.

6. Jesus dies

O Saviour of the world . . .

Read carefully St Mark chapter 15 verses 33 to 39

(Pause to think about the reading)

Why has God allowed it to happen?
The cry of a mother seeing her son die —
a young life wasted!
The cry of a good man who has given all
and seems to have lost everything.
My God, my God, why have you forsaken me?
The cry of Jesus whose own life seems to have ended
    in failure.
There seems no convincing answer to tragedy.
It seems utterly meaningless — a waste!
And yet, Jesus, you are there with those who ask the
    question.
You are still there in the darkness even when we
    cannot see or hear you.

You have given everything to me, even your life.

7. Jesus is risen

O Saviour of the world . . .

Read carefully St Mark chapter 16 verses 1 to 8

(Pause to think about the reading)

You bring good out of evil;
light out of darkness;
life out of death.
Death seems like the end,
but it releases new possibilities.
The seed dies before it bursts into flower.
Change and growth are only possible where there is
    first dying.

Help me Lord, to look beyond what is dying,
to look beyond death,
to what is new and fresh.

Thank you for making all things new each day.
Thank you for being alive and with us now.

(You could conclude with the prayer of St Francis, St Teresa or St Richard. See pages 55–57)

A note on meditation

Meditation is a form of reflective prayer requiring very few words. Sometimes you may feel that you just want to be quiet in God's presence. Many people however, probably need to have a sentence from scripture or from some other source with which to focus their attention.

You can use a phrase or a sentence which appeals to you in a prayer, a psalm or in your scripture reading. You may also find suitable material in poetry or in other books.

First, read over the phrase or passage you have chosen, concentrate on it, and spend some time thinking about what it is saying.

Second, think how it applies specifically to you.

Third, ask yourself if it suggests something you might do in response to it. It may lead to silent worship, praise, or thanksgiving, or it might lead to some practical action or concern.

Some famous prayers

St Francis of Assisi (1181–1226)

Lord, make me an instrument of your peace.
Where there is hatred, let me sow love;
where there is injury, pardon;
where there is doubt, faith;
where there is despair, hope;
where there is sadness, joy;
where there is darkness, light.

O Divine Master, grant that I may not so much
seek to be consoled, as to console;
not so much to be understood, as to understand;
not so much to be loved, as to love.
For it is in giving that we receive;
it is in pardoning that we are pardoned;
it is in dying that we are born again to eternal life.

St Richard of Chichester (1197–1253)

Thanks be to you, my Lord, Jesus Christ,
for all the benefits which you have given me,
for all the pains and insults which you have borne
    for me:

O most merciful Redeemer, Friend and Brother;
may I know you more clearly,
love you more dearly,
and follow you more nearly,
day by day.

St Ignatius Loyola (1491–1556)

Teach us, good Lord, to serve you as you deserve;
to give and not to count the cost;
to fight and not to heed the wounds;
to toil and not to seek for rest;
to labour and not to ask for any reward,
but the knowledge that we do your will;
through Jesus Christ our Lord. Amen.

St Teresa of Avila (1515–82)

You have no body on earth but ours,
no hands but ours,
no feet but ours;
ours are the eyes
showing your compassion to the world;
ours are the feet with which you go about doing good;
ours are the hands with which you are to bless us now.

Sir Francis Drake (1540–96)

O Lord God, when you entrust your servants with any
great matter, grant us also to know that it is not the
beginning, but the continuing of the same to the end,
which yields the true glory; through him who for the
finishing of your work laid down his life, our Redeemer,
Jesus Christ. Amen.

Sarum Primer (1558)

God be in my head and in my understanding;
God be in my eyes and in my looking;
God be in my mouth and in my speaking;
God be in my heart and in my thinking;
God be at my end and at my departing.

Some more prayers

The Holy Spirit

We cannot see the wind blowing;
we can only see the trees bending in its path;
we can only see the ripples stirring the surface of the
water.

We cannot see your Spirit, Lord,
but only the movement in people's lives caused by
your love.
Breathe on me and stir up the lethargy of my concern.
Breathe on me and kindle the dying embers of love.
Breathe on me and awaken me to new life.

The Way, the Truth, and the Life

Loving Father, give me faith in this dark world to
walk with your Son, Jesus Christ who is the Way.
Give me simplicity amidst the confusion around me to
learn from him who is the Truth; and give me courage
to entrust myself completely to him who is the Life; so
shall I possess that life which is found in him alone.

The Christian Way

Help me, Lord, to make my way through this world in peace with good courage, holding fast to all that is good. May I never repay evil with evil, but always support and strengthen those who are weak and help those in need; and may I always love and serve you cheerfully rejoicing constantly in the power of the Holy Spirit.

(Based on a blessing in the 1928 Prayer Book)

Home and family

Thank you Lord, for the comfort and security of my home, and the love and concern of my family. Help me not to take all this for granted, but to take my full share in the responsibilities which need to be borne. And may this home always reflect the love and peace of your eternal kingdom.

For the sick

Father, you want all men and women to be whole. Comfort and heal all who are sick or in pain, and give courage and hope to the dying. Give skill to doctors and nurses, and all who tend the sick. Increase our knowledge of mental and physical disease so that they can be treated more effectively. And give to each one of us that hope and faith without which we can never know true wholeness.

Science and Technology

Man has come of age.
We have skills and knowledge
never dreamt of before.
Our environment is at our control,
and we can benefit so much from scientific research.
We thank you, Lord, for progress,
but realize that so often
we have not the responsibility or maturity
to use these gifts.
Help us to grow spiritually
and always use them for good,
and not for our destruction.

God in every man

Father, I find it easy to criticize,
to find fault, to see the wrong in others,
and it blinds me to the shortcomings of my own life.
Help me to see the good things, the best in people,
for in everyone there is the seed of your Spirit.

(George Fox in his Journal wrote: 'Walk cheerfully over
this world answering that of God in every one'.)

Index of Prayers